j520 BUTTERFI
Butterfield, Moira, 1
Space.

SPACE

MOIRA BUTTERFIELD AND PAT JACOBS

Cavendish Square

New York

Published in 2016 by Cavendish Square Publishing, LLC
243 5th Avenue, Suite 136, New York, NY 10016

First Edition

Website: cavendishsq.com

This publication represents the opinions and views of the author based on his or her personal experience, knowledge, and research. The information in this book serves as a general guide only. The author and publisher have used their best efforts in preparing this book and disclaim liability rising directly or indirectly from the use and application of this book.

CPSIA Compliance Information: Batch #CW16CSQ

All websites were available and accurate when this book was sent to press.

Cataloging-in-Publication Data

Butterfield, Moira.
Space / by Moira Butterfield and Pat Jacobs.
p. cm. — (Know it all)
Includes index.
ISBN 978-1-5026-0884-0 (hardcover) ISBN 978-1-5026-0882-6 (paperback) ISBN 978-1-5026-0885-7 (ebook)
1. Astronomy — Juvenile literature. 2. Solar system — Juvenile literature. I. Butterfield, Moira, 1960-. II. Title.
QB46.B88 2016
520—d23

Project managed and commissioned by Dynamo Limited
Consultants: Sally Morgan, Dr. Patricia Macnair, Brian Williams, Carey Scott, Dr. Mike Goldsmith.
Authors: Moira Butterfield and Pat Jacobs
Editor / Picture Researcher: Dynamo Limited
Design: Dynamo Limited

KEY – tl top left, tc top center, tr top right, cl center left, c center,
cr center right, bl bottom left, bc bottom center, br bottom right.
All photographs and illustrations in this book © Shutterstock except: cover, 1 PlanilAstro/Shutterstock.com, Corbis 26cl Ye Shuhong/Xinhua Press, 26bc Ye Shuhong/Xinhua Press; Mark A. Garlick 5bl, 6l, 7c, 7r, 10, 11, 12c, 13, 14c, 15t, 15c, 16t, 17t, 18, 19, 20t; MBA STUDIOS 25c; NASA 4tr WMAP Science Team, 4l ESA/G. Illingworth/D. Magee/P. Oesch (University of California, Santa Cruz)/R. Bouwens (Leiden University)/HUDF09 Team, 4br WMAP Science Team, 5t Nick Wright UCL/IPHAS Collaboration, 5r NOAO/ESA/the Hubble Helix Nebula Team/M. Meixner (STScI)/ T.A. Rector (NRAO), 9 Far-infrared: ESA/Herschel/PACS/SPIRE/Hill, Motte, HOBYS Key Programme Consortium; X-ray: ESA/XMM-Newton/ EPIC/XMM-Newton-SOC/Boulanger, 12l SDO, 13b Johns Hopkins University Applied Physics Laboratory/Carnegie Institution of Washington, 14b, 16tl JPL-Caltech/MSSS, 16cr JPL-Caltech/Cornell/Arizona State Univ., 16b JPL-Caltech/Cornell/U.S. Geological Survey, 17l JPL 17cr JPL/ DLR, 18l JPL, 19b JPL/USGS, 20tl Halley Multicolor Camera Team, Giotto Project/ESA, 20bl JHUAPL, 21l, 21c JPL-Caltech, 21r, 22 JPL-Caltech, 22l, 23t, 23b, 24l, 24r, 24b, 25b, 26t, 26c Donald Walter (South Carolina State University)/Paul Scowen and Brian Moore (Arizona State University).

Printed in the United States of America

Table of Contents

The Universe 4

Stars 5

Galaxies 6

The Milky Way 7

A Star Nursery 8

The Solar System 10

Solar System Secrets 11

The Sun 12

Mercury and Venus 13

Our Earth 14

The Moon 15

Mars 16

Jupiter and Saturn 17

Uranus and Neptune 18

Dwarf Planets 19

Comets and Asteroids 20

Exploring Space 21

Space Travel 22

The International Space Station 24

Inside a Spacesuit 25

Looking into Space 26

Space Mysteries 27

Glossary 28

Further Information 30

Index 31

The Universe

The universe is everything in space, including many billions of stars and planets, moons, and asteroids. Nobody knows for sure how far it stretches.

The universe begins

The universe is thought to be around 13.7 billion years old. Its birth is sometimes called the "Big Bang." According to the Big Bang theory, the universe began with a sudden expansion of space, which was packed with energy and extremely hot. The universe has continued to expand and cool ever since. As it very slowly cooled, gases formed, followed by stars and planets. The Big Bang was so powerful that its effects are still being felt. Clusters of stars found in space are still moving outward, scattering apart.

Scientists think the universe might be round, saddle-shaped, or flat.

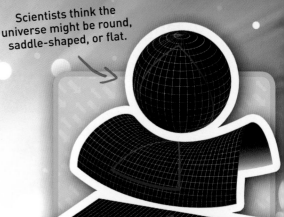

The shape of the universe

Scientists have different theories about the shape of the universe. Some think it could be ball-shaped. Others think it could be flat or curved like a horse's saddle. They disagree about what might eventually happen to the universe, too. There are theories that in many billions of years all the stars might burn out or the universe could even rip apart. Ideas regularly change as we discover new things about deep space (faraway space).

The size of the universe

Nobody knows how large the universe is. We know only that, using powerful space telescopes, we can see light that is about 13.7 billion light-years away. This is the edge of what is called the "observable" universe, but there may be more light coming from farther away that hasn't had time to reach us yet. Some scientists think there might even be more than one universe.

Hot shots!

A BABY UNIVERSE

This image of deep space shows one of the farthest parts of the universe that we have seen. It is so far away that the light from it took about 13.7 billion years to reach Earth. It is a snapshot of the universe near to the time when it was born.

Stars

Stars are gigantic balls of gas that give out heat and light. New ones are forming and old ones are dying all the time. The sun is our nearest star.

When stars are born

Stars are born in huge, swirling clouds of gas called nebulae. A star forms when part of a nebula begins to shrink, growing hotter and starting to spin. It is sometimes possible for a space telescope to spot signs of a hot, newborn star when the star heats up the gas in the nebula around it and makes it glow (shown right).

Dwarfs and giants

Stars are different sizes and different colors, too, because they burn at different temperatures. The biggest ones, called supergiants, are hundreds of times bigger than our sun and burn much more brightly. White dwarfs are the smallest and are no bigger than Earth. Bluish-white stars are hottest, followed by white, yellow, orange, and red. The coolest stars are too dim to see.

A red dwarf star

A yellow dwarf star

The scale of a yellow dwarf star (like our sun) compared to giant stars

A red giant star

A blue giant star

A red supergiant star

When stars die

Stars die when they run out of fuel to burn. In the case of a slow-burning red dwarf star, this can take many billions of years, but fiercely burning supergiants die more quickly. When average-sized stars like our sun finally start to run out of fuel, they expand to become a red giant. After that they may fade away or explode in a spectacular supernova.

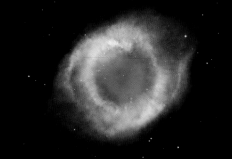

Galaxies

A galaxy is a giant collection of stars, gas, clouds and dust clouds. There are thought to be billions of galaxies in the universe, with billions of stars and planets in each galaxy, too. Galaxies themselves are usually found in groups called clusters.

1 Lenticular galaxy

2 Elliptical galaxy

3 Irregular galaxy

4 Barred spiral galaxy

5 Spiral galaxy

⬊ Know your galaxies

There are five main galaxy shapes:

1. Like a lens: A lenticular galaxy has a bulging center surrounded by a flat disk and consists mostly of old stars.

2. Old star's home: Elliptical galaxies are round or slightly oval. They are made up of older stars and seem to have few or no new stars.

3. Messy youngsters: Irregular galaxies have no distinctive shape. They are quite small and have lots of gas, dust, and young stars.

4. The shape we're in: A barred spiral galaxy has arms coming out of a bar shape with a core in the middle. Our galaxy, the Milky Way, is this type.

5. Pinwheel-style: A spiral galaxy has several arms swirling around a central core. The core contains bright older stars, and the arms are filled with young stars and gas clouds.

Black holes

Many galaxies are thought to have a black hole at the center—a point in space where gravity is so strong that it sucks in everything nearby. Nothing, not even light, can escape. A black hole is thought to form when a huge star explodes and the leftover core collapses in on itself.

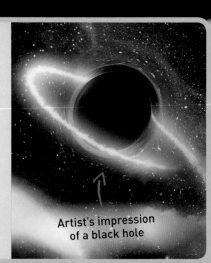

Artist's impression of a black hole

The Milky Way

Our galaxy, the Milky Way, has between 200 and 400 billion stars orbiting around its center, along with many billions of planets. Our sun and solar system are located in one of its spiral arms.

What is the Milky Way made of?

The Milky Way is so named because the part of it that we can see looks rather like milk spilled across the sky. The whole of the galaxy measures about 100,000 light-years across (many trillions of miles). Along its spiral arms lie stars, planets, and clouds of dust and gas, but in its center there is thought to be a supermassive black hole.

The Milky Way seen from Earth

Location of the sun in the Milky Way

Stars visible April to July in the Northern hemisphere

stars

lines defining constellations

Lyra
Hercules
Cornona Borealis
Canes Venatici
Bootes
Ophiuchus
Serpens
Scorpius
Libra
Virgo
Lupus
Corvus
Centaurus
Crux
Milky Way

The constellations

Since ancient times people have joined up the stars they can see in the night sky to make shapes called constellations. Earth's night side faces different parts of the sky at different times of the year, as it goes around the sun, so you will see different constellations throughout the year. Sky maps such as the one shown above show constellations appearing in the night sky at different times of the year. People in other parts of the world give their own names to the constellations. For instance, in the Marshall Islands in the North Pacific they call the Great Bear constellation a canoe instead.

💡 Know it all!

● The nearest galaxy to the Milky Way is Andromeda. It is about 2.5 million light-years away, but the two galaxies are moving toward each other at around 310,686 miles (500,000 km) per hour. Eventually they will collide, though this will take many billions of years.

Spinning around and speeding on

Our solar system is rotating around the central core of the Milky Way, just like all the other stars and planets in the galaxy. It takes the sun around 225 million years to go all the way around the center once. As it spins around, the whole of the Milky Way is moving through space at roughly 373 miles (600 km) a second.

The big picture!

A Star Nursery

This beautiful image shows part of the Eagle Nebula in one of the arms of the Milky Way. Inside this gigantic gas cloud, stars are being born.

Part of the Eagle Nebula is nicknamed the "pillars of creation." The image of the pillars was taken by the Hubble Telescope orbiting above Earth's atmosphere. Its sensors gathered data such as the infrared light coming from the cloud. The data was analyzed by computers to create the finished picture, and colors were added to make it easier to see.

 Know it all!

● The tallest "pillar of creation" in the Hubble image towers an immense four light-years high.

● Dense blobs of gas break off the pillars, and stars grow inside the blobs. Our own solar system probably formed this way.

● The gas and dust in the nebula is lit by young stars being born in its depths.

● The ancient Greeks called the Milky Way the "Milky Circle." The ancient Romans called it the "Milky Road." They had no idea they were looking at part of a giant galaxy.

● Stars do not really twinkle. They only appear to shimmer because the light they emit wobbles as it travels through Earth's atmosphere to reach us.

● The nearest star to our sun is Proxima Centauri. It is a red dwarf star about 4.24 light-years away.

The "pillars of creation," finger-like areas of the nebula where stars are being born

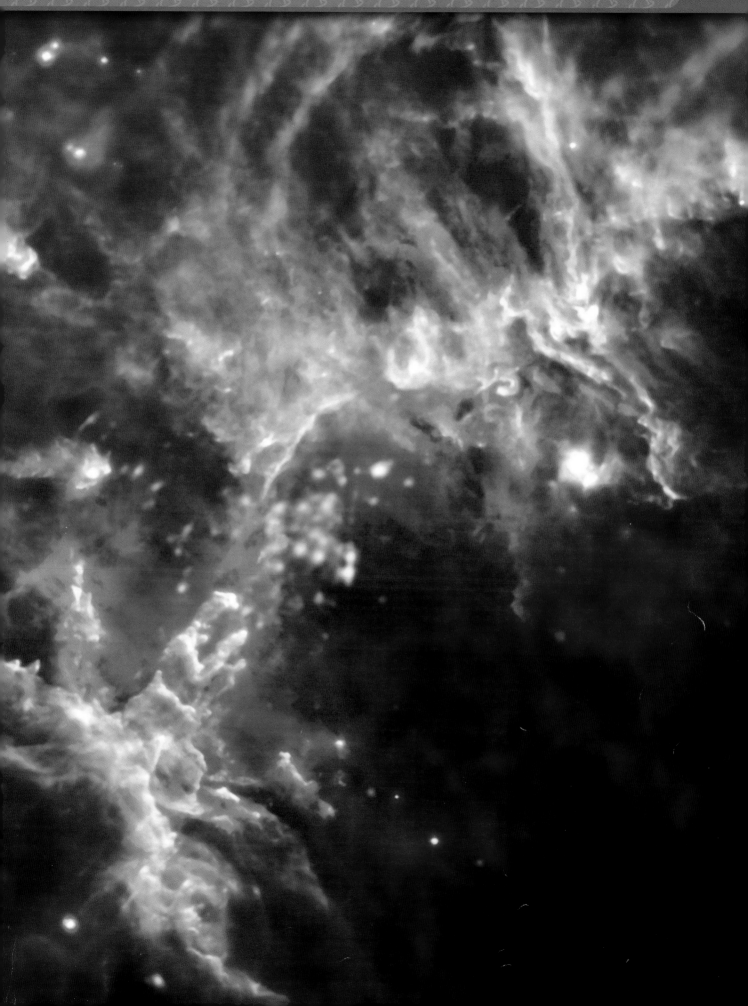

The Solar System

Our Earth is one of a group of planets that orbit the sun. Moons, asteroids, comets, and dwarf planets go around the sun, too. Together the whole group is called the solar system.

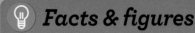 *Facts & figures*

● More than 160 moons orbit the eight planets of the solar system. New ones are still being discovered.

● There are billions of comets and asteroids in the solar system.

What's in the Solar System?

There are eight major solar system* planets, including Earth, along with smaller worlds called dwarf planets. There are also a vast number of rock and metal lumps called asteroids, most of them orbiting in a region called the asteroid belt between Mars and Jupiter. Farther out, past all the planets, there is a region of icy floating fragments called the Kuiper Belt. Farthest away is an outer region of comets and dust called the Oort Cloud.

Venus · Mars · Saturn · Uranus

Mercury · Earth · Jupiter · Neptune

*PLANETS ARE NOT SHOWN TO SCALE

Held by the Sun

The sun's gravity—its pulling force—holds all the objects in the solar system in place. Their speed around the sun stops objects from falling toward it, while the pull of the sun stops them flying off into space. The more mass (matter) an object has, the more powerful the force of its gravity. The sun has far more mass than anything else in the solar system.

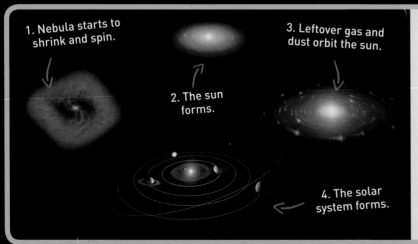

1. Nebula starts to shrink and spin.

2. The sun forms.

3. Leftover gas and dust orbit the sun.

4. The solar system forms.

The birth of the solar system

The solar system formed around five billion years ago inside a nebula cloud of dust and gas. Part of the nebula started spinning as it shrank and heated up, forming the sun. Leftover gas and dust formed the planets. Rocky planets are closest to the sun. Planets of gas and ice are farther away.

Solar System Secrets

The solar system is so vast that we are still not certain exactly what there is to find at its edges. Unmanned space probes are only now reaching those distant parts and sending back information. Here are some of the facts we can be sure of.

Hot and cold

The planets closest to the sun are the hottest. So while the average temperature on Earth is 59 degrees Fahrenheit (15 degrees Celsius), Venus has a scorching-hot average of 867°F (464°C). Meanwhile, faraway Uranus has an unimaginably cold average temperature of –330°F (–201°C). Gas giants have no reachable solid surface, so space probes measure their temperature at the top of the gas clouds surrounding them.

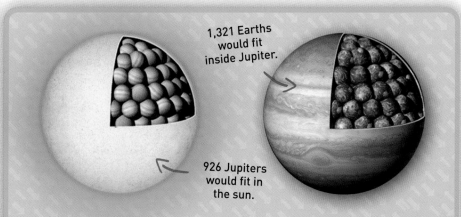

1,321 Earths would fit inside Jupiter.

926 Jupiters would fit in the sun.

Planet sizes

The eight major planets come in two size categories—gas giants and small rocky planets. Jupiter is the biggest gas giant, and Earth is the biggest rocky planet. To give you some idea of the vast difference in sizes, more than 1,300 Earths would fit into the size of Jupiter, and 926 Jupiters would fit into the size of the gigantic sun. Dwarf planets are the smallest, and there may be more of these still to discover.

Venus 867°F

Mercury 846°F
(day side)

Earth 59°F *(average)*

Mars –81°F

Jupiter –162°F

Saturn –218°F

Neptune –323°F

Uranus –330°F

Orbit and spin

Solar objects orbit the sun, and they spin, too. Earth takes one year to orbit the sun and one twenty-four-hour day to spin around on its axis (an imaginary line through Earth between the North and South poles). Planets that are farther away take longer to go around the sun. For instance, the journey takes distant Uranus eighty-four Earth years. As they travel, different planets spin at different rates, too. For instance, Saturn spins faster than Earth and its day lasts just 10.6 hours.

💡 Know it all!

● In our solar system, you would weigh more on planets with a bigger mass than Earth because they would have a stronger gravitational pull on you. You would weigh less on smaller planets and moons because their gravitational pull would be weaker than Earth's.

Jupiter has more than twice the mass of the other planets put together.

The Sun

...e sun is a superhot ball of ...drogen gas. The hydrogen ...ts fuel. The sun contains ...ough hydrogen to shine on ... another five billion years.

...perhot surface

...e sun's surface is made ...bubbling gas churning ...ound at 9,932°F (5,500°C). ...s changing all the time. ...lar storms sometimes ...upt and giant solar flares ...pear, shooting storms of ...rticles high above the surface. ...metimes patches of gas cool ...ghtly, creating dark-looking ...gions called sunspots that grow ...nd shrink. The sun is so massive ...at these seemingly small-looking ...unspots can often be much wider ...an Earth.

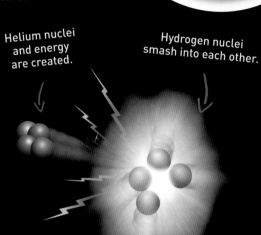

Helium nuclei and energy are created.

Hydrogen nuclei smash into each other.

Sun's superpower

The sun isn't actually on fire, like a piece of wood might be on Earth. It gets its heat from superhot hydrogen nuclei (particles of matter) smashing into each other deep in its core. They create helium nuclei and give off energy, in a process called nuclear fusion.

 Know it all!

● In ancient times people worshipped the sun as a god. In ancient Greece the sun god was called Apollo.

● Astronomers can only study the sun using very specialized equipment. Never look directly at the sun yourself because you could badly damage your eyesight.

Solar winds coming our way

Particles stream out from the sun in a constant solar wind ("solar" means "of the sun"). This blast of magnetically charged particles blows in all directions and, when solar flares erupt on the sun's surface, extra-big gusts of particles shoot across the solar system. If lots of them reach Earth they can even disrupt radio communications, and at the North and South poles they trigger beautiful sky displays called auroras (shown above).

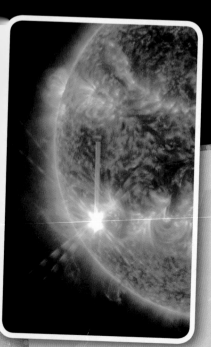

Hot shots!

⭐ **FLARE UP**

This is an image captured by special sun-monitoring equipment, showing a solar flare as it erupts from the superhot surface of the sun.

Mercury and Venus

Mercury is the nearest planet to the sun, followed by Venus.
Both are barren, hellish planets where life is unlikely to survive.

Moonlike Mercury

Mercury is an airless, dry world rather like our moon. Its surface is covered with craters where asteroids have collided with it. Cliffs, sometimes .6 to 2.5 miles (1 to 4 km) high, run across the surface between highland areas and vast, flat, pockmarked plains. By day, its temperature is unbelievably hot, but by night it is freezing.

Hellish Venus

Venus has a deadly-poisonous atmosphere ninety times denser than Earth's—so dense that it would crush any object that tried to land. The atmosphere is made of carbon dioxide and clouds of sulphuric acid. These stinking, yellowish clouds trap heat, making the planet even hotter than Mercury. Huge volcanoes tower above the plains of Venus, which may once have been running with rivers of liquid sulphur.

Flying by

Unmanned space probes have been sent to study the inner planets. From 2008 to '09 and beyond, NASA's space probe *Messenger* flew above Mercury's surface three times and took images of its crater-covered surface (shown right). It flew past Venus and took images of that, too.

💡 Facts & figures

● Mercury measures 3,032 miles (4,879 km) across.

● Venus is 7,521 miles (12,104 km) across.

● One day on Mercury is as long as 58.6 Earth days.

● One day on Venus is as long as 243 Earth days.

Our Earth

Earth is the third planet away from the sun and the only planet in the solar system known to have liquid water on its surface. It is a rocky world with a molten metal core.

Spinning and turning

It takes twenty-four hours for Earth to spin around on its axis, and while one-half of the planet experiences daytime, the other half experiences nighttime. As Earth turns, the sun appears in different positions in the sky. Earth takes 365.25 days to orbit around the sun. That extra 0.25 of a day is the reason we put an extra day into the calendar every four years, in a "leap year." If we didn't add the extra day, our calendar would eventually get out of step with the seasons.

Facts & figures

- Earth's diameter is 7,926 miles (12,756 km).
- It is 93 million miles (150 million km) from the sun.
- Its surface temperature ranges from –126°F to 136°F.
- It is around 4.6 billion years old.

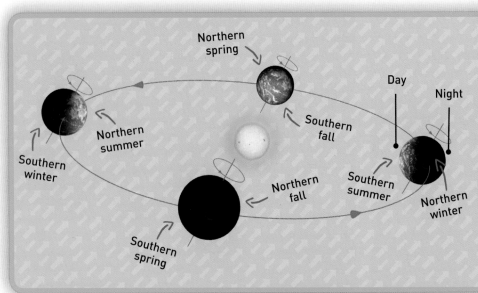

Northern spring

Southern fall

Northern summer

Southern winter

Day   Night

Southern summer

Northern fall

Northern winter

Southern spring

Seasons in the Sun

Earth is tipped over on its axis, causing the seasons as the planet orbits the sun. For half the year Earth's northern half—the Northern Hemisphere—tips toward the sun and experiences spring and summer. Meanwhile the Southern Hemisphere has fall and winter. Gradually the seasons are reversed.

Hot shots!

FIRST VIEW

This is the first color picture ever seen of Earth from space. It was taken on Christmas Eve 1968, by US Apollo astronauts, and it amazed the world.

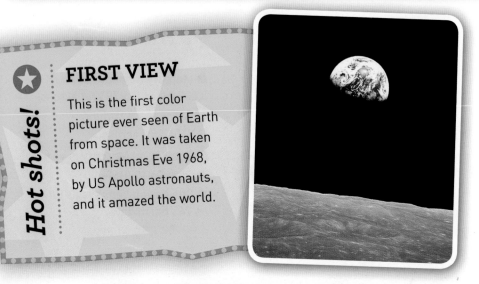

One of a kind?

Scientists call Earth a "Goldilocks" planet because it isn't too hot or too cold, giving just the right conditions for liquid water and life to exist. It is in the "Goldilocks Zone"—just the right distance from its star, the sun. Astronomers have identified other possible Goldilocks planets orbiting other stars. They might possibly have liquid water and perhaps even life!

The Moon

The moon is a rocky, airless sphere orbiting Earth. It is a dry, barren place, yet it has a great effect on us, causing (along with the sun) the tides on our planet.

A small planet smashes into Earth.

The debris from the impact. This eventually formed the moon.

The moon orbits Earth.

Birth of the Moon

Scientists think that soon after Earth formed in space it was hit by another small planet. Debris scattered around Earth and eventually formed into the moon. Analysis of moon rock collected by astronauts backs up the theory that the moon is made of Earth debris.

The surface of the moon

Most of the moon's surface is rough, mountainous highlands, pitted with craters formed when asteroids, meteoroids, or meteorites crashed into the surface. When we look at the moon's surface from Earth, its highland areas appear pale and its large flat plains appear as darker patches. The moon does not have soil on its surface. Instead it has fine, powdered rock.

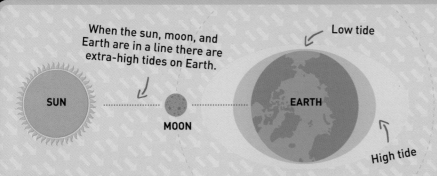

When the sun, moon, and Earth are in a line there are extra-high tides on Earth.

Low tide

SUN

MOON

EARTH

High tide

Pulling on our planet

The moon's gravity tugs on Earth and on the oceans, too. It has the effect of raising the oceans in two bulges on opposite sides of the planet. As Earth turns, these bulges move, causing the tides. Sea level rises and falls twice a day, creating high and low tides. When the moon, Earth, and sun are in a line, the gravitational pull of the sun and the moon work together to create extra-high tides called spring tides.

 Know it all!

● Twelve astronauts have walked on the moon, all taking part in US Apollo space missions. When they returned to Earth they left behind equipment on the surface, which is still there.

● The astronauts also left their footprints in the moon's dust. The footprints will be there still, too, as there is no wind on the moon to blow them away.

Mars

Mars is the fourth planet away from the sun in the solar system. It is a rocky world with a metal core like Earth's, but its surface is very different.

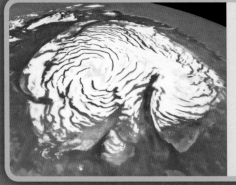

Was Mars watery?

Mars is a bitterly cold place. Any water on the planet is frozen, and there are ice caps at its South and North Poles (shown left). However, evidence gathered by unmanned space probes suggests that Mars was once warm enough to have flowing water, possibly salty lakes and seas. It seems as though Mars might once have been a warmer and wetter place, perhaps more like Earth.

Probing Mars

Unmanned space rovers have been roaming Mars, exploring its craters, plains, volcanoes, and canyons. Their analysis of rock samples suggests that there may once have been simple forms of water-based life on Mars, though we can't be sure yet. Varying levels of methane gas have been measured in the atmosphere of the planet, too, which has led scientists to suggest that some type of bacterial life might still exist below the planet's surface, producing the methane.

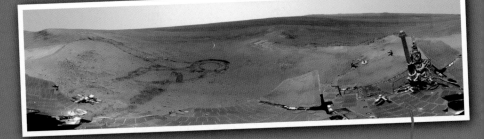

An image of the surface of Mars taken by a Mars Rover space probe

A poisonous place

Mars has an atmosphere made up of carbon dioxide, which is toxic. Whirlwinds regularly rip across its plains, and giant dust storms last up to a month on its surface. The dust on Mars is red-colored because it is made of iron oxide—what we call rust.

Hot shots!

WATER ROCKS

This *Mars Rover* shot of Mars shows types of small, round rock that form in liquid water, suggesting that Mars was once a wetter and warmer place.

Jupiter and Saturn

Jupiter and Saturn are gas giants—planets made almost entirely of gas, with no surface to land on. They are much bigger than the inner rocky planets of the solar system.

Biggest on the block

Jupiter is the solar system's biggest planet and has the most moons. It spins around very fast, whipping its deadly-poisonous gas clouds into raging storms. It has one particularly massive storm that has been raging for centuries and is called the "Great Red Spot." The image of it above was taken by an uncrewed spacecraft.

Io

Europa

Ganymede

Callisto

Amazing moons

Jupiter's four largest moons are called Ganymede, Callisto, Io, and Europa. All four are larger than our moon, and probes show them to be fascinating, strange places. Ganymede has lots of volcanoes and is shrouded in poisonous sulphur gas. Io is possibly the most volcanic spot in the whole solar system, with giant volcanoes and lava lakes. Callisto and Europa are icy, though they may have oceans beneath their frozen crusts.

💡 Know it all!

● Jupiter's Great Red Spot storm rages over an area 14,913 miles (24,000 km) wide.

● Jupiter and Saturn spin around incredibly fast. Jupiter's day lasts just 9.9 hours, and Saturn's day lasts 10.6 hours.

● New moons are still being discovered circling these giant gas planets.

Rings of ice

Gas giant Saturn is famous for its rings, clearly visible through telescopes on Earth. The rings are made of orbiting ice particles, some as small as snowflakes and others as big as giant boulders. The Cassini-Huygens space probe (pictured right) has been orbiting Saturn, exploring its stormy cloud cover and many moons. These include the strange world of Titan—Saturn's largest moon. It has giant rivers and lakes of methane and is shrouded in smog. It is the only moon in the solar system with a planet-like atmosphere.

⊚Uranus and Neptune

Uranus and Neptune are the icy, cold, outer planets in the solar system. They are called the "ice giants."

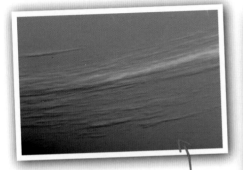

Clouds of gas on Neptune

Slushy spots

Uranus and Neptune seem to be made mostly of a slushy mixture of ice, hydrogen, and helium gases. Both planets are very stormy. Neptune is the windiest planet in the solar system, with gusts of up to 1,491 miles per hour (2,400 kmh). The strongest winds ever recorded on Earth are around 230 mph (370 kmh).

Knocked sideways

Uranus rotates on its side, at a different angle to all the other planets in the solar system. At some time in its early history it may have been in a collision with a large object that knocked it over onto its side. It takes eighty-four years to orbit the sun, so each of its seasons lasts twenty-one years. That means parts of the planet face away from the sun for decades.

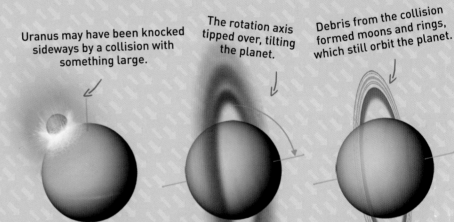

Uranus may have been knocked sideways by a collision with something large.

The rotation axis tipped over, tilting the planet.

Debris from the collision formed moons and rings, which still orbit the planet.

Many moons

Both Uranus and Neptune have icy rings and moons. One of Neptune's moons, called Triton, has huge geysers of liquid nitrogen that shoot up from its surface and probably rain down nitrogen frost across the planet's surface. Many of the moons in this far region of the solar system are mysterious places we know little about. New moons are regularly being discovered.

💡 *Know it all!*

● Uranus was given the name Georgium Sidus when it was first discovered in 1789.

● Uranus and Neptune look bluish, partly because the methane gas in their atmospheres absorbs the red part of the sun's light but reflects the blue part.

Dwarf Planets

The dwarf planets are a collection of mostly small, icy worlds at the edge of the solar system, mainly in the area called the Kuiper Belt.

A long, long birthday wait

Unlike the major planets, which have circular orbits, the dwarf planets make highly elliptical (oval-shaped) orbits around the sun, taking centuries to get around. Sedna, the farthest dwarf planet so far discovered in the solar system, takes 10,500 years to orbit the sun once. A year on Pluto lasts 248 Earth years.

Pluto the mini planet

Pluto was once called a planet, but it is actually smaller than our own moon. It has five mini moons of its own, including Charon, Nix, and Hydra. These cold, icy worlds can only be seen dimly by space telescopes. A spacecraft flew past them in 2015 and sent back close-up views and measurements. Pluto's surface has mountains and is mostly covered in methane and nitrogen ice.

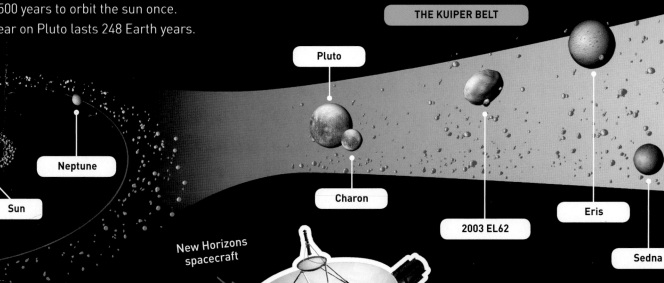

THE KUIPER BELT

Pluto

Neptune

Sun

Charon

2003 EL62

Eris

Sedna

New Horizons spacecraft

Probes far away

In 2006, NASA launched the *New Horizons* spacecraft to Pluto. The dwarf planet is billions of miles away. The craft reached Pluto on July 2015 and mapped its surface features, worked out what it is made of and what its atmosphere is like. After viewing Pluto, *New Horizons* went on to view some other Kuiper Belt objects, too.

Facts & figures

● Pluto is 3.7 billion miles (5.9 billion km) from the sun.

● One day on Pluto is as long as 6.39 Earth days.

● Its average surface temperature is thought to be around −382°F (−230°C).

Comets and Asteroids

Comets and asteroids sometimes visit our skies as they speed on their way around the sun. Occasionally, fragments of space rock even crash-land on our planet.

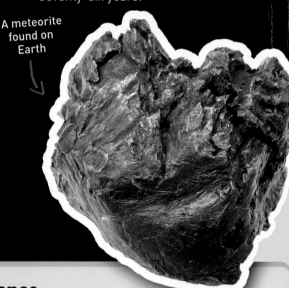

Snowballs in space

Comets are giant lumps of dirty ice orbiting in the solar system. Their journey sometimes takes them close to the sun. When this occurs they begin to give off a cloud of gas and dust that is blown into two long tails— one dust, one gas—by solar winds. Some comets appear regularly in the skies above Earth and have names, such as Halley's Comet, which appears every seventy-five to seventy-six years.

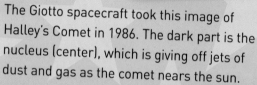

Hot shots!

★ **HALLEY'S SECRET CENTER**

The Giotto spacecraft took this image of Halley's Comet in 1986. The dark part is the nucleus (center), which is giving off jets of dust and gas as the comet nears the sun.

A meteorite found on Earth

Earth visitors

Meteoroids are rocky space fragments that are smaller than asteroids. Sometimes one enters Earth's atmosphere and burns up as it falls, briefly blazing in the sky as a meteor. If it falls to Earth's surface it is called a meteorite (shown right). Meteorites vary from tiny, dust-sized fragments to pieces as big as a boulder. Thousands fall to Earth every year.

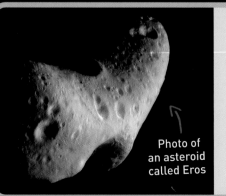

Photo of an asteroid called Eros

Floating potato shapes

Asteroids are irregular-shaped rock and metal lumps that range in size. Many hundreds of thousands orbit in the asteroid belt between Mars and Jupiter, but some pass close to Earth on their journey. In 2010, Japan's Hayabusa spacecraft landed on an asteroid called Itokawa and returned to Earth with some asteroid dust to analyze. Itokawa turned out to be a stony S-type asteroid.

Exploring Space

Exploring space takes years of planning and a great deal of money and expertise.

Human exploration

So far, humans have traveled as far as the moon. From 1969 to 1972 the US Apollo program regularly landed astronauts there for visits of a few days. Since then astronauts have lived in space stations orbiting Earth, working out how to survive in space for months at a time. This may lead to a manned mission to Mars, perhaps in around 2025. A crewed spacecraft would take several months to reach Mars.

The Voyager 1 space probe, which reached the outer solar system

Mars rover *Curiosity* on the surface of Mars

Uncrewed exploration

Unmanned probes are more practical for visiting far-flung and extremely dangerous parts of the solar system to take measurements and samples. They are bristling with antennae, lenses, and sensors to collect data. They are not usually designed to return to Earth, but they transmit home all the information they collect.

Escaping from Earth

To escape Earth's gravity, spacecraft and satellites are fitted on top of powerful rockets, which fire them into space and put them into orbit. The rocket drops away from the spacecraft and re-enters Earth's atmosphere, usually landing in the ocean. Launch rockets are propeled by giant tanks of fuel. When ignited, the fuel burns to produce gases that rush out of engine nozzles, pushing the rocket upward.

💡 Know it all!

● It takes only minutes for a launch rocket to use up its entire fuel supply because it burns up vast quantities of fuel each second.

Follow the facts!

Space Travel

Follow the arrows to discover some of the
most important dates in the
history of space travel.

1965

The Soviet cosmonaut
Alexei Leonov performs
the first ever
space walk.

1963

The Soviet cosmonaut
Valentina Tereshkova
becomes the first
woman in space.

1961

The Soviet cosmonaut
Yuri Gagarin becomes
the first man
in space.

1986

The space shuttle
Challenger explodes
shortly after liftoff,
killing all seven
astronauts.

1988

Work begins on
building the ISS—the
International Space
Station.

2000

The first resident crew lives on
board the ISS, which
orbits Earth.

💡 Know it all!

● Dogs and chimpanzees
were placed into rockets and
blasted into orbit in early space
travel experiments, before the
technology was tried on humans.

1969

US *Apollo 11* lands the first men on the moon.

1971

The Soviet Union launches the first successful space station, Salyut 1.

1972

The date of the last Apollo mission, and the last time anybody walks on the moon.

1981

The first flight of the American space shuttle *Columbia*.

1986

The Soviet Union launches its space station, Mir (the Russian word for "peace").

2011

The last ever space shuttle mission. *Atlantis* delivers crew and supplies to the ISS.

Know it all!

● US astronaut Neil Armstrong (above) was the first person to step onto the moon, followed by his colleague, Buzz Aldrin.

● Space tourism is about to take off. Spaceplanes will carry passengers on trips to the edge of space and back, to experience weightlessness.

● Like most of the early astronauts, Yuri Gagarin, the first person in space, was a trained pilot. He died in a jet plane crash in 1968.

🪐 The International Space Station

A space station is a spaceship orbiting Earth. Astronauts can visit it and stay for a while before returning home. The biggest one built so far is the International Space Station—the ISS for short.

The ISS in orbit around Earth. It is roughly the size of a soccer field.

Built big

The ISS was built in space by astronauts from many different countries working together. It took many deliveries of crew and equipment from Earth and hours of spacewalking before the station was ready for a long-term crew in 2000. The finished station is made up of modules—different sections—fitted together.

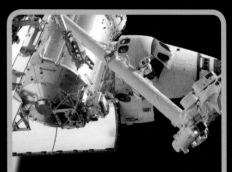

Space station sections

The ISS is powered by giant solar panels, which convert the sun's light into electricity. It has several science labs for space experiments, as well as living quarters for seven crew members. Every few months a spacecraft arrives from Earth to bring new supplies. The image above shows a visit from a US space shuttle.

💡 Facts & figures

● The ISS cost around $96 billion—the most expensive single object ever built.

● The living and working quarters are the equivalent of the space in two big passenger jet aircrafts.

● The ISS orbits Earth once every ninety minutes.

● Nearly 8 miles (13 km) of wiring connects the power systems.

Living on board

The crew must get used to working and living in zero gravity. They float and so do all the other objects on board. To sleep they must strap themselves to the wall of the station, and they must be careful not to drop anything, such as a tool or some food for example, because it could float away and damage the station equipment. Zero gravity affects the human body and muscles start to waste away, so the crew members must do two hours of exercise every day to work their muscles (right).

Inside a Spacesuit

When astronauts go spacewalking they must wear a spacesuit, which acts as their own mini spaceship. Without it they would very swiftly die.

Staying comfortable

The spacesuit provides oxygen to breathe and water to drink. The underwear layer contains tubes that circulate cooling water around the astronaut's skin. Astronauts wear a space diaper, so if they need to go to the toilet when they are outside, they can go in their suit. The backpack supplies oxygen and power and takes away the carbon dioxide breathed out by the astronaut.

Staying safe

NASA spacesuits, called EMUs, have eleven layers of cloth and foil, giving a spacewalking astronaut protection from searing sunshine, freezing cold, and the sun's radiation. For half of a ninety-minute orbit spacewalkers are in darkness, so they need lights on their helmets. For half the time they are in bright sunlight, so they need a helmet visor coated with gold to block dangerous ultraviolet rays.

Staying in contact

Inside the helmet there is a cap fitted with earphones and a microphone for staying in contact with other astronauts and with Earth. Astronauts can adjust communication, temperature, oxygen flow, and lights using the control panel on the chest pack. A tether connects them safely to their spaceship. Without it they would float off into space!

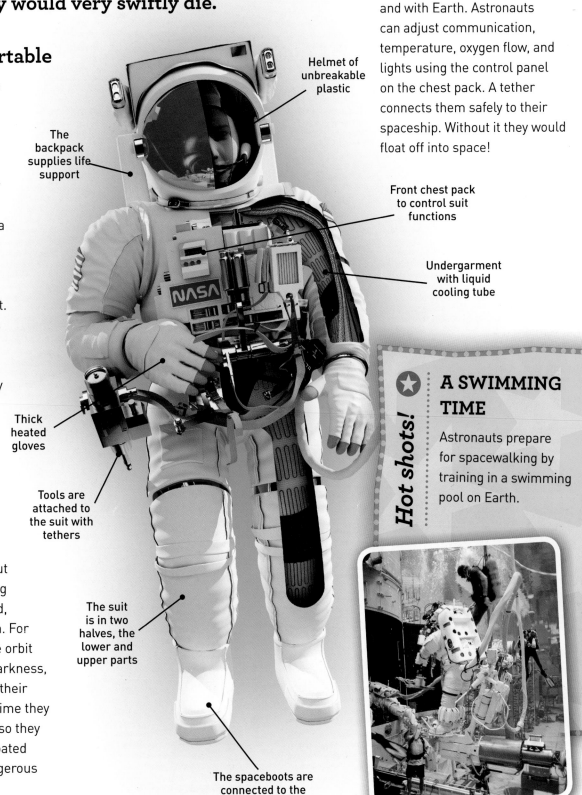

Helmet of unbreakable plastic

The backpack supplies life support

Front chest pack to control suit functions

Undergarment with liquid cooling tube

Thick heated gloves

Tools are attached to the suit with tethers

The suit is in two halves, the lower and upper parts

The spaceboots are connected to the legs of the suit.

Hot shots!

A SWIMMING TIME

Astronauts prepare for spacewalking by training in a swimming pool on Earth.

Looking into Space

Telescopes work by gathering more light than a human eye ever could. They collect and measure light coming from objects in space.

On the ground

A telescope captures light and directs it via mirrors to measuring instruments. Ground-based space telescopes have giant mirrors housed inside buildings that open to the sky. They are built in isolated areas of the world where the sky is most likely to be clear, dry, and unpolluted. One of the largest, the VLT (Very Large Telescope) is in the Atacama Desert in northern Chile, where there is very little cloud cover to obscure the view.

Above Earth

Orbiting space telescopes get a better view than those on the ground because they fly high above Earth's atmosphere, which distorts and blocks the light coming from space. The Hubble Space Telescope, launched in 1990, has provided hundreds of thousands of amazing space images that have helped astronomers to find answers to mysteries such as the age of the universe. The James Webb Space Telescope is set to do an even better job.

The James Webb Space Telescope is roughly the size of a tennis court.

The Hubble Space Telescope saw far into deep space.

Looking for light

Space telescopes carry equipment for examining light in different ways. They detect the different wavelengths (parts) of light and energy radiation that an object in space might emit, such as ultraviolet, infrared, X-rays, and gamma rays. This data can be used to analyze features such as an object's temperature, what it is made of, and its size.

The VLT (also shown below) has mirrors up to 28 feet (8.5 m) across.

💡 *Know it all!*

● The Hubble Space Telescope orbits 354 miles (569 km) above Earth. The James Webb Space Telescope is set to orbit 932,507 miles (1.5 million km) above Earth, getting an even better view of deep space.

⊘ Space Mysteries

Space telescopes have helped astronomers to look at some amazing space secrets. Here are some incredible examples of what they have found.

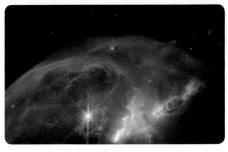

↑ Space bubble

Stars are born in swirling clouds of gas called nebulae. This dramatic-looking bubble occurs between a star and the gas cloud of the nebula around it.

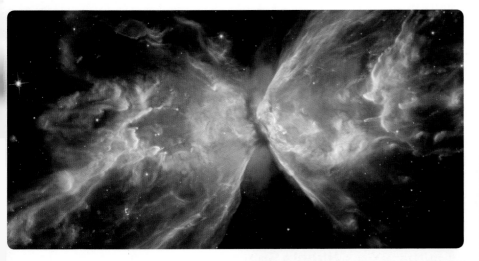

↑ Butterfly nebula

Space images can be very beautiful. The butterfly-shaped nebula above is actually the last gasp of a dying star system.

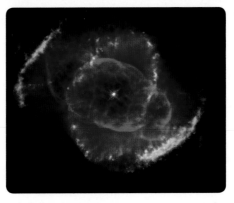

↑ Galaxy pileup

Four galaxies merge together in a massive space crash above. Space telescopes have revealed lots of galaxy collisions.

↑ Glowing eye

Hubble took the image above, showing a cloud of glowing gas called a planetary nebula, the wreckage of an exploded star.

↑ See a supernova

Supernova 1987A, the mega-explosion at the death of a massive star is seen here surrounded by the gas and stars of a galaxy.

💡 Know it all!

● Space telescopes have led to some very puzzling discoveries. One of the most mysterious is the apparent presence of "dark energy" in the universe, something unseen that makes up a large part of space and affects the behavior of galaxies. One thing is for certain: when it comes to space, we definitely do NOT know it all!

Glossary

Andromeda The nearest galaxy to our own. Andromeda is spiral-shaped.

Apollo A series of US space missions to the moon between 1968 and 1975.

Asteroid An irregular-shaped lump of rocky, metallic material orbiting a star.

Asteroid belt A region between Mars and Jupiter where lots of asteroids orbit the sun.

Atmosphere A layer of gases around the surface of a planet, moon, or star.

Aurora A display of natural light in the sky, caused by electromagnetic particles near the Earth's North and South poles.

Big Bang A sudden expansion of space, thought to have created the universe around 13.7 billion years ago.

Black hole A region of space where the force of gravity prevents everything, even light, from escaping.

Comet A big lump of dust and ice orbiting the sun. When a comet nears the sun it develops streaming trails of gas and dust.

Constellation A pattern of stars.

Cosmonaut The Russian word for an astronaut.

EMU A spacesuit (the letters stand for Extravehicular Mobility Unit).

Galaxy A large group of stars along with their planets, moons, asteroids, and comets.

Gamma rays A type of energy radiation given off by some objects in space.

Gas giant A planet that is made mostly of gases, with only a small solid core.

Goldilocks planet A planet that is the right temperature for life to exist on it.

Gravity A force of attraction (a pulling force) between objects.

Hubble Space Telescope A space telescope launched in 1990 to orbit Earth looking outwards at space.

ISS The International Space Station, which orbits Earth, providing a home for astronaut crews.

Kuiper Belt A region of our solar system farther away than the planets, where lots of icy lumps orbit the sun.

Light-year The distance that light travels in a year. One light-year is nearly 5.9 trillion miles (9.5 trillion km).

Meteor A bright streak that appears in the sky when a small fragment of rock called a meteoroid enters Earth's atmosphere.

Meteorite The name given to a meteoroid (small fragment of space debris) if it lands on Earth.

Milky Way The name of the galaxy that contains Earth, the sun, and all the planets in the solar system, along with many other stars and planets.

Moon A large, ball-shaped object that orbits a planet.

NASA The US National Aeronautics and Space Administration, which organizes space travel and space exploration.

Nebula A giant space cloud of gas and dust.

Nuclear fusion When two tiny particles join and release energy. Stars are fueled this way.

Oort Cloud A region of comets thought to be in the far reaches of the solar system.

Orbit A journey that takes a continual path around and around something.

Radiation Energy that comes out from something. Light and heat are both types of radiation.

Red dwarf A type of star that is quite small and cool compared to larger, hotter stars.

Sensor A piece of equipment set up to transmit a signal when it senses something. The signals it sends can be measured, and its data is sometimes used to create images.

Sky map A map of the night sky showing the constellations (groups of stars) that can be seen on a clear night.

Solar system The sun and all the planets, moons, asteroids, and comets that orbit it.

Solar wind A stream of high-speed particles that shoot off the sun.

Space probe A spacecraft sent from Earth to explore objects in space more closely.

Space station A spacecraft with living and working quarters for astronauts, who can come and go from Earth.

Space telescope A satellite that gathers light from space, using mirrors to focus it and create an image.

Space tourism A privately funded journey into space.

Star A giant ball of burning gases.

Sunspot A slightly cooler spot on a star's superhot surface.

Zero gravity When something is floating and seemingly weightless.

Further Information

BOOKS

Aguilar, David A. *Space Encyclopedia: A Tour of Our Solar System and Beyond*. National Geographic Kids. Des Moines, IA: National Geographic Kids Books, 2013.

Carney, Elizabeth. *National Geographic Readers: Planets.* Des Moines, IA: National Geographic, 2012.

Devorkin, David H., and Robert Smith. *Hubble: Imaging Space and Time*. Reprint edition. Des Moines, IA: National Geographic, 2011.

Dinwiddie, Robert, Heather Couper, John Farndon, Nigel Henbest, David Hughes, David Sparrow, Carol Stott, and Colin Stuart. *The Planets*. New York. DK, 2014.

Simon, Seymour. *The Sun*. New York: HarperCollins, 1989.

WEBSITES

Discovery's Space News

news.discovery.com/space

Articles, videos, and photos from Discovery Communications cover a vast range of subjects.

Space and NASA News

www.space.com

Get news, photographs, webcasts, and amazing articles straight from the source, the National Aeronautics and Space Administration.

Index

Page numbers in **boldface** are illustrations. Entries in **boldface** are glossary terms.

Aldrin, Buzz, 23
Andromeda, 7
Apollo, 14–15, 21, 23
Armstrong, Neil, 23, **23**
asteroid belt, 10, 20
asteroids, 4, 10, 13, 15, 20, **20**
astronauts, 14–15, 21–25, **24**, **25**
Atlantis, 23
atmosphere, 8, 13
aurora, 12

Big Bang, 4
black hole, 6–7, **6**
blue giant, **5**

Cassini-Huygens, 17, **17**
Challenger, **22**
Columbia, 23, **23**
comets, 10, 20
constellations, 7, 7
cosmonaut, 22

dark energy, 27
dwarf planets, 10, 19

Eagle Nebula, 8, **8–9**
Earth, 4–5, 8, 10–16, **10**, **11**, **14**, **15**, 18–22, 24–26
    about, 14
    rotation and orbit of, 14
    seasons on, 14

EMU, 25

Gagarin, Yuri, 22–23, **22**
galaxies, 6–8, **6**, 27, **27**
    types of, 6
gamma rays, 26
gas giants, 11, 17
Goldilocks planet, 14
gravity, 6, 10, 15, 21, 24

Halley's comet, 20, **20**
Hubble space telescope, 8, 26–27, **26**
hydrogen, 12, 18

ice giants, 18
ISS (International Space Station), 22, **22**, 24, **24**

James Webb space telescope, 26, **26**
Jupiter, 10–11, **10**, **11**, 17, **17**, 20
    Great Red Spot, 17
    moons of, 17

Kuiper Belt, 10, 19, **19**

Leonov, Alexei, 22
light-years, 4–5, 7–8

Mars, 10, **10**, 11, 16, **16**, 20–21
Mars rover, 16, **16**, **21**
Mercury, **10**, 11, 13
Messenger, 13
meteor, 20
meteorite, 15, 20, **20**
Milky Way, 6–8, **7**

moons, 4, 10, 19
  of Jupiter, 17, 17
  our moon, 13, 15, **15**, 17, 19, 21, 23
  of Neptune, 18
  of Saturn, 17
  of Uranus, 18

NASA, 13, 25
nebula, 5, **5**, 8, **8**, 10, **10**, 27, **27**
Neptune, **10**, 11, 18, **18**
New Horizons, 19, **19**
nuclear fusion, 12

Oort cloud, 10
orbit, 7–8, 10–11, 14–15, 17–22, 24–26

"pillars of creation," 8, **8**
planets, 4, 6–7, 10–11, 13–14, 16–19
  dwarf planets, 10, 19
  size of, 11
  temperature of, 11
Pluto, 19, **19**
Proxima Centauri, 8

radiation, 25–26
red dwarf, 5, **5**, 8
red giant, 5, **5**
rockets, 21–22, **21**

Saturn, **10**, 11, 17, **17**
sensor, 8, 21
sky map, 7, **7**
solar system, 7–8, 10–12, **10**, 14, 16–21
  birth of, 10
solar wind, 12

space exploration, 21–23
space probes, 11, 13, 16–17, 19, 21, **21**
space shuttle, 22–24, **23**, **24**
space station, 22–24
spacesuit, 25, **25**
space telescope, 5, 19, 26–27, **26**
space tourism, 23
stars, 4–7, **5**, **27**
  birth of, 5, 8, 27
  death of, 5, 27
  types of, 5
sun, 5, 7, 10–16, **10**, 18–20, **19**, 24–25
sunspots, 12
supergiant, 5, **5**
supernova, 5, 27

Tereshkova, Valentina, 22
tides, 15

universe, 4, **4**, 6, 27
  beginning of, 4
  shape of, 4
  size of, 4
Uranus, **10**, 11, 18, **18**

Venus, **10**, 11, 13
VLT (Very Large Telescope), 26, **26**
Vogayer 1, **21**

white dwarfs, 5

yellow dwarf, **5**

zero gravity, 24